W9-BJG-826

DATE DUE			

THURGOOD MARSHALL

By Barbara M. Linde

Gareth Stevens
Publishing

Please visit our website, www.garethstevens.com. For a free color catalog of all our high-quality books, call toll free 1-800-542-2595 or fax 1-877-542-2596.

Library of Congress Cataloging-in-Publication Data

Linde, Barbara M.
Thurgood Marshall / Barbara M. Linde.
    p. cm. — (Civil rights crusaders)
Includes index.
ISBN 978-1-4339-5700-0 (pbk.)
ISBN 978-1-4339-5701-7 (6-pack)
ISBN 978-1-4339-5698-0 (library binding)
1. Marshall, Thurgood, 1908-1993—Juvenile literature. 2. Judges—United States—Biography—Juvenile literature. 3. African American judges—Biography—Juvenile literature. 4. United States. Supreme Court—Biography—Juvenile literature. I. Title.
KF8745.M34L56 2011
347.73'2634—dc22
[B]
                                2011012803

First Edition

Published in 2012 by
Gareth Stevens Publishing
111 East 14th Street, Suite 349
New York, NY 10003

Copyright © 2012 Gareth Stevens Publishing

Designer: Katelyn E. Reynolds
Editor: Kristen Rajczak

Photo credits: Cover, pp. 3–24, back cover (background) Shutterstock.com; cover, pp. 1, 19 Bachrach/Getty Images; pp. 5, 7 Hank Walker/Time & Life Pictures/Getty Images; p. 9 Keystone/Getty Images; p. 11 New York Times Co./Getty Images; p. 13 Hulton Archive/Getty Images; p. 15 Ed Clark/Time & Life Pictures/Getty Images; p. 17 Sam Falk/New York Times Co./Getty Images.

Printed in the United States of America

CPSIA compliance information: Batch #CS11GS: For further information contact Gareth Stevens, New York, New York at 1-800-542-2595.

CONTENTS

Words in the glossary appear in **bold** type the first time they are used in the text.

WORKING FOR CIVIL RIGHTS

Thurgood Marshall was an important **civil rights** leader. He was a judge and the first black Supreme Court justice. All his life, he fought **discrimination** and **segregation**. He once said, "A child born to a black mother in a state like Mississippi . . . has exactly the same rights as a white baby born to the wealthiest person in the United States."

Thurgood believed in using the court system to gain civil rights for African Americans. Justice and equality were his main goals.

LET FREEDOM RING

The Supreme Court is the highest court in the United States. The court's nine justices decide some of the country's most important cases.

Thurgood stands in front of the Supreme Court building in Washington, DC.

EARLY LIFE

Thoroughgood Marshall was born July 2, 1908, in Baltimore, Maryland. In second grade, he shortened his name to Thurgood. He lived in an **integrated** neighborhood but attended segregated schools.

Thurgood sometimes got into trouble in elementary school. Each time he did, he had to learn part of the US **Constitution** by heart. After high school, Thurgood went to Lincoln University in Pennsylvania. He was skilled at arguing and getting others to agree with him. He used these qualities to become a **lawyer**.

LET FREEDOM RING

Thurgood married Vivian "Buster" Burey in 1929. They were married until she died in February 1955. He married Cecilia Suyat in December 1955.

Cecilia and Thurgood had two sons,
Thurgood Jr. and John.

Cecilia Suyat

LAW SCHOOL

Thurgood attended the all-black Howard University Law School in Washington, DC. He learned a lot from a teacher named Charles Hamilton Houston. Charles believed the Constitution gave the same rights to all people, but laws weren't always applied equally.

In the late 1800s, some Southern states passed laws that said segregation was legal if blacks had equal places or opportunities. In 1896, the Supreme Court even said "separate but equal" was legal. Charles and Thurgood said separate wasn't equal.

LET FREEDOM RING

Thurgood believed the Constitution's **amendments** made it a fairer "document of freedom."

Thurgood graduated from Howard in 1933. He was the top student in his class.

▽

9

FIRST LAW PRACTICE

Thurgood opened his law practice in Baltimore and stayed in touch with Charles. Charles worked with the **NAACP**.

In 1935, Charles helped Thurgood win a court case for the NAACP. The segregated University of Maryland Law School had turned down a student just because he was black. Thurgood proved this was illegal segregation because there wasn't an "equal" law school for blacks in the state. The school was then required to accept African American students.

LET FREEDOM RING

Thurgood had wanted to attend the University of Maryland. He couldn't because of segregation.

Thurgood speaks to the press about a Supreme Court decision in 1955.

THE NAACP

Thurgood and Charles both began working full time for the NAACP. In 1940, Thurgood helped create the NAACP Legal Defense Fund. For more than 20 years, Thurgood led this team of lawyers who helped poor blacks. They took on segregation and discrimination cases. Thurgood's likable manner and talent as a storyteller helped him win over white **juries** and judges.

Thurgood himself presented 32 cases to the Supreme Court. He won 29 of them. Little by little, African Americans began to gain equality.

LET FREEDOM RING

During one Supreme Court case, a justice asked Thurgood what the word "equal" meant. Thurgood said, "Equal means getting the same thing, at the same time, and in the same place."

Thurgood receives an award from NAACP executive secretary Roy Wilkins in 1964.

A MAJOR WIN

In 1953, Thurgood presented a case called *Brown v. Board of Education* to the Supreme Court. He argued that segregation was against the Constitution and separate schools weren't equal. Schools for black students often didn't have books, desks, or other supplies. Schools for white students did. Black teachers were paid less than white teachers. Many knowledgeable people supported Thurgood in court.

On May 17, 1954, all the Supreme Court justices agreed—school segregation had to end.

LET FREEDOM RING

Twenty-one states had segregated public schools. Some of them refused to integrate after *Brown v. Board of Education*. However, Thurgood won another Supreme Court case, which said they had to integrate quickly.

Brown v. Board of Education was one of many cases that challenged segregation. Here, Thurgood speaks about it in 1958.

FEDERAL JUDGE

By 1961, Thurgood was well known for his civil rights victories in the courts. President John F. Kennedy made him a judge on the **US Court of Appeals**. Sometimes the cases he heard were taken all the way to the Supreme Court. The Supreme Court often agreed with his decisions on the cases.

In 1965, President Lyndon B. Johnson made Thurgood the solicitor general. That meant he was now the lawyer for the US government. From 1965 until 1967, Thurgood argued 19 cases before the Supreme Court. He won 14 of them.

LET FREEDOM RING

Thurgood was just the second African American to become a federal judge. He was the first African American to become solicitor general.

Thurgood sits at his desk in Washington, DC, shortly after becoming solicitor general.

SUPREME COURT JUSTICE

On October 2, 1967, Thurgood became the first African American Supreme Court justice. President Johnson had appointed him. Thurgood supported civil rights for African Americans, women, and other **minority groups**. Equality in education was still one of his main goals. Thurgood was often able to get the other justices to agree with him.

By 1991, Thurgood's health was failing. He left his job on the Supreme Court. Thurgood died in 1993 in Bethesda, Maryland. His memorial service was shown on television.

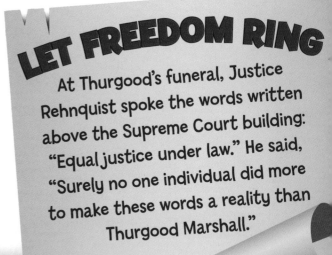

LET FREEDOM RING

At Thurgood's funeral, Justice Rehnquist spoke the words written above the Supreme Court building: "Equal justice under law." He said, "Surely no one individual did more to make these words a reality than Thurgood Marshall."

Thurgood served on the Supreme Court for almost 24 years.

IN MEMORY

Thurgood Marshall's civil rights efforts have been remembered. In 1980, the University of Maryland named its new law library for him. His statue stands in front of the Baltimore courthouse. Scholarships and student court contests are named for him.

Thurgood once said, "None of us got where we are solely by pulling ourselves up by our bootstraps. We got here because somebody . . . bent down and helped us pick up our boots." "Mr. Civil Rights" certainly helped many African Americans make their way to equality.

TIMELINE

1908 Thurgood Marshall is born on July 2 in Baltimore, Maryland.

1933 Thurgood graduates from Howard University Law School.

1935 Thurgood wins his first big case against the University of Maryland.

1940 Thurgood helps create the NAACP's Legal Defense Fund.

1954 Thurgood wins the Supreme Court case *Brown v. Board of Education*.

1961 Thurgood becomes a judge on the US Court of Appeals.

1967 Thurgood is appointed to the US Supreme Court.

1991 Thurgood retires from the Supreme Court.

1993 Thurgood dies.

GLOSSARY

amendment: a change or addition made to a legal document

civil rights: the freedoms granted to US citizens by law

Constitution: the laws that govern the United States

discrimination: treating people differently because of race or beliefs

integrated: a place or organization open to all races

jury: a group of people chosen to decide a court case

minority group: people who are not part of the main group of a society. In the United States, African Americans, Native Americans, Latinos, and the poor are minority groups.

lawyer: a person whose job it is to handle people's problems and questions about the law

NAACP: the National Association for the Advancement of Colored People, a civil rights organization founded in 1909

segregation: the forced separation of races or classes

US Court of Appeals: the second-highest federal court. Lawyers appeal, or ask the court to reconsider, decisions from lower courts.

FOR MORE INFORMATION

Books

Adler, David A. *Heroes for Civil Rights*. New York, NY: Holiday House, 2008.

Whitelaw, Nancy. *Thurgood Marshall*. Greensboro, NC: M. Reynolds Publishing, 2011.

Websites

Stand Up for Your Rights
pbskids.org/wayback/civilrights
Learn more about your civil rights and the people who fought for them.

Thurgood Marshall: Civil Rights Advocate
www.socialstudiesforkids.com/articles/ushistory/thurgoodmarshall1.htm
Read about Thurgood Marshall's life and work as a lawyer.

INDEX